The Future of Money: Navigating Wealth in the Age of Innovation

E. M. Brooks

Foreword

Money has always been more than a medium of exchange—it is a mirror reflecting the complexities of human civilization. From the first bartered goods to the emergence of centralized banking systems, money has evolved in tandem with technology, governance, and societal structures. Today, as we stand on the precipice of the most significant financial transformation in history, the very nature of money is once again being reshaped. The convergence of artificial intelligence, blockchain technology, digital currencies, and sustainability initiatives heralds a new era of financial systems, one filled with both unprecedented opportunities and profound uncertainties.

This book is not merely an exploration of trends; it is a guide to understanding and navigating the tectonic shifts reshaping our financial landscapes. By blending rigorous research, practical insights, and a forward-looking perspective, it aims to equip readers with the tools to thrive in a world where the boundaries of money are constantly being redefined.

The chapters ahead will unravel the layers of this transformation, from the promise and perils of decentralization to the ethical dilemmas of an increasingly financialized society. Whether you are an investor, policymaker, entrepreneur, or curious thinker, this journey will illuminate the paths leading to the future of money.

Contents

Chapter 1: Introduction: The New Meaning of Money — 1

Chapter 2: The Cashless Society: Myths and Realities — 5

Chapter 3: Central Bank Digital Currencies (CBDCs): The State Strikes Back — 11

Chapter 4: Decentralized Finance (DeFi): A Revolution or a Bubble? — 17

Chapter 5: Artificial Intelligence and Financial Decision-Making — 23

Chapter 6: Global Inequality and the Future of Wealth Distribution — 29

Chapter 7: Green Finance and the Push for Sustainability — 33

Chapter 8: The Tokenized Economy: Beyond Currency — 38

Chapter 9: Hyperinflation and the Risks of a Digital-Only World — 43

Chapter 10: The Philosophy of Money: Value Beyond Economics — 49

Chapter 11: Financial Inclusion in the Age of Technology — 55

Chapter 12: Ethics and Innovation in Financial Systems — 61

Chapter 13: The Intersection of Globalization and Financial Systems   69

Chapter 14: The Role of Trust in the Future of Financial Systems   77

Chapter 15: Financial Resilience in an Era of Uncertainty   85

Afterword   93

Chapter 1: Introduction: The New Meaning of Money

Money is as old as civilization itself, yet its essence has always been in flux. Over millennia, societies have devised countless forms of currency, from the barter systems of prehistory to the complex digital assets of today. Each transformation has mirrored the technological capabilities, economic priorities, and cultural values of the era in which it occurred. Today, as technology accelerates at an unprecedented pace, the concept of money is undergoing a radical metamorphosis, one that will redefine not only financial systems but also the very fabric of human interaction.

At its core, money fulfills three primary functions: it is a medium of exchange, facilitating trade by eliminating the inefficiencies of barter; a store of value, preserving wealth over time; and a unit of account, providing a standard measure for valuing goods and services. Yet, these utilitarian definitions fail to capture the deeper societal role of money. It is also a social contract, a shared belief system that assigns value to otherwise inert materials—whether shells, metal coins, or digital bits.

This duality of money—its tangible utility and its intangible social essence—has made it both a stabilizing force in economies and a source of immense volatility. The history of money is, in many ways, a history of human civilization: a tale of innovation, conflict, cooperation, and adaptation.

The Evolution of Money: A Brief Historical Context

The story of money begins with the barter system, a rudimentary yet functional means of trade that dominated early human societies. While barter allowed for the direct exchange of goods and services, it suffered from inefficiencies, particularly the "double coincidence of wants." If a farmer needed tools but the blacksmith required grain, trade could only occur if both parties coincidentally desired what the other offered.

To overcome these limitations, ancient societies introduced commodity money—items such as salt, grain, and precious metals that held intrinsic value and were widely accepted as mediums of exchange. Over time, the intrinsic value of money became less important than its perceived value, leading to the emergence of representative money, such as gold-backed currencies, and eventually fiat money, whose value derives solely from government decree.

The 20th century saw the rise of global financial institutions, centralized banking systems, and multinational corporations, all of which reinforced the dominance of fiat currencies. Yet, this centralized model of money also created vulnerabilities. The global financial crisis of 2008, for instance, exposed the fragility of traditional banking systems and catalyzed a wave of innovation that continues to reshape the financial landscape today.

The Digital Revolution and the New Financial Order

The 21st century marks a turning point in the evolution of money, driven by advances in technology and shifting societal values. The digital revolution has given rise to entirely new forms of money, from cryptocurrencies like Bitcoin and Ethereum to central bank digital currencies (CBDCs). These innovations challenge traditional notions of trust and authority, decentralizing financial power and enabling peer-to-peer transactions on a global scale.

Cryptocurrencies, built on blockchain technology, offer a glimpse into a future where money is not tied to nation-states but to networks. Bitcoin, for instance, was designed as a deflationary currency immune to the inflationary pressures of fiat money. Ethereum expanded the possibilities by introducing programmable money through smart contracts, enabling automated transactions without intermediaries. While these innovations hold immense potential, they also raise questions about regulation, security, and accessibility.

CBDCs, on the other hand, represent the state's response to the rise of decentralized currencies. Governments around the world, from China to the European Union, are experimenting with digital versions of their national currencies. These initiatives aim to combine the efficiency of digital transactions with the stability of centralized control, but they also pose challenges related to privacy and surveillance.

Beyond Technology: The Ethical and Societal Dimensions

While technology is a key driver of change, the future of money is not solely a technological story. Ethical considerations, geopolitical dynamics, and environmental sustainability are equally critical. For instance, the energy consumption of cryptocurrency mining has sparked debates about the environmental impact of digital currencies. Meanwhile, the potential for digital money to exacerbate inequality or facilitate financial exclusion cannot be ignored.

Geopolitically, the rise of digital currencies has implications for global power dynamics. Bitcoin's decentralized nature challenges the dominance of the US dollar as the world's reserve currency, while China's digital yuan represents a strategic move to expand its influence in international trade.

On a societal level, the shift toward digital money raises questions about privacy and individual autonomy. In a cashless society, every transaction is potentially traceable, creating opportunities for both financial transparency and state surveillance. How do we balance the benefits of digital efficiency with the need to protect individual freedoms?

A Glimpse into the Future

As we look ahead, it is clear that the future of money will be shaped by the intersection of technology, society, and economics. Innovations such as quantum computing, artificial intelligence, and tokenized economies will continue to push the boundaries of what is possible, while societal pressures for inclusion, sustainability, and equity will demand new frameworks and solutions.

The chapters that follow will explore these themes in detail, offering a comprehensive examination of the forces transforming money in the 21st century. By understanding the past and present, we can better prepare for a future where money is not just a tool for trade but a reflection of human ambition, creativity, and resilience.

Chapter 2: The Cashless Society: Myths and Realities

The dream of a cashless society, where physical currency is replaced entirely by digital transactions, has captured the imagination of governments, businesses, and consumers alike. Advocates argue that a world without cash would bring unparalleled convenience, efficiency, and transparency. Critics, however, warn of significant risks, from heightened surveillance to the exclusion of vulnerable populations. As societies edge closer to this reality, it becomes crucial to dissect the promises and perils of abandoning cash.

A cashless society is not a new concept. Early proponents of digital payments envisioned a utopia where technological innovation would eliminate inefficiencies in traditional monetary systems. Today, advancements in mobile payments, digital wallets, and blockchain technology have brought this vision within reach. Yet, the transition is fraught with challenges, raising questions about who benefits from a cashless world and at what cost.

The Evolution of Digital Payments

The journey toward cashlessness began long before the rise of modern digital wallets. In the mid-20th century, the introduction of credit cards marked a significant shift in how people made payments, reducing dependence on cash. Debit cards and electronic bank transfers further expanded the scope of cashless transactions, paving the way for online shopping and e-commerce in the 1990s.

The early 21st century saw the proliferation of mobile payment platforms, from PayPal to Apple Pay, which allowed users to conduct transactions via smartphones. These innovations were quickly embraced in regions like Scandinavia, where robust digital infrastructure and high trust in financial institutions facilitated the rapid decline of cash usage. Sweden, often cited as the pioneer of cashlessness, now reports that fewer than 10% of its transactions involve cash.

The rise of central bank digital currencies (CBDCs) has further accelerated the push toward a cashless society. Unlike cryptocurrencies, which operate on decentralized networks, CBDCs are state-issued digital currencies designed to function as legal tender. By combining the efficiency of digital payments with the stability of traditional monetary systems, CBDCs aim to provide a bridge between the old and the new.

Advantages of a Cashless Economy

Proponents of cashless systems highlight several compelling benefits. For consumers, digital payments offer unparalleled convenience. Transactions can be completed instantaneously from anywhere in the world, eliminating the need to carry physical currency or visit a bank. For businesses, cashlessness reduces operational costs associated with handling and storing cash, while improving security by minimizing theft and fraud.

Governments also stand to gain from cashless systems. Digital transactions leave a detailed trail, making it easier to track economic activity and reduce tax evasion. Transparency in financial flows can aid in combating money laundering, corruption, and illicit trade. In developing economies, mobile payment platforms have enabled financial inclusion for millions of unbanked individuals, empowering them to participate in the global economy.

The Risks and Challenges of Cashlessness

Despite these advantages, the transition to a cashless society is not without significant drawbacks. Critics argue that abandoning cash risks deepening social inequalities and eroding fundamental rights. One of the most pressing concerns is the exclusion of vulnerable populations. Elderly individuals, low-income households, and those in rural areas often lack access to the digital infrastructure required for cashless transactions. Without careful planning, these groups risk being marginalized in a cashless world.

Privacy is another critical issue. Digital payments generate vast amounts of data, which can be used to track consumer behavior, monitor financial activities, and even suppress dissent in authoritarian regimes. While transparency can deter criminal activity, it also creates opportunities for surveillance and abuse. The question of who controls this data and how it is used remains contentious.

Furthermore, digital systems are inherently vulnerable to cyberattacks. A cashless economy depends on secure networks to function, but recent years have seen an increase in ransomware attacks, data breaches, and financial fraud. The centralization of digital payment platforms creates single points of failure, amplifying systemic risks in the event of technological disruptions.

Global Case Studies: Successes and Failures

The shift toward cashlessness has unfolded unevenly across the globe. In countries like Sweden and Denmark, cash is rapidly becoming obsolete. These nations benefit from strong digital infrastructure, high trust in financial institutions, and social policies designed to include vulnerable populations in the transition. Sweden's Riksbank has even proposed issuing a digital krona to ensure public access to legal tender in a cashless future.

In contrast, nations with less robust infrastructure have struggled with cashless initiatives. India's demonetization in 2016, aimed at reducing corruption and encouraging digital payments, led to widespread economic disruption. Small businesses, dependent on cash transactions, suffered significant losses, while rural populations faced severe hardships due to inadequate access to banking and internet services.

China presents a unique case study. Mobile payment platforms like Alipay and WeChat Pay dominate the country's financial ecosystem, making cash increasingly redundant. However, this dominance has raised concerns about monopolistic practices and the potential misuse of financial data by the state. The launch of China's digital yuan adds another layer of complexity, blending the efficiency of digital payments with centralized control.

Ethical and Philosophical Implications

The push toward a cashless society raises profound ethical questions. What does it mean to live in a world where every transaction is traceable? How do we balance the benefits of transparency with the need for privacy and autonomy? Cash has long been a symbol of individual freedom, allowing anonymous transactions and financial independence. Its disappearance could mark a shift toward greater state and corporate control over personal finances.

Moreover, the environmental impact of digital payments warrants scrutiny. While cash production has its own carbon footprint, the energy demands of digital payment systems—particularly those reliant on blockchain—are far from negligible. As societies adopt cashless systems, they must also grapple with their ecological consequences.

The Road Ahead

The vision of a cashless society is both exhilarating and daunting. Its realization will depend on how governments, businesses, and individuals address the challenges of inclusion, privacy, and security. Technological innovation alone cannot create a just and equitable financial system; it must be guided by ethical considerations and inclusive policies.

As we move closer to a world without cash, it is essential to remain vigilant about the potential pitfalls and unintended consequences. A cashless society has the power to transform economies, improve efficiencies, and foster innovation—but only if its implementation is thoughtful, inclusive, and grounded in principles of equity and justice.

Chapter 3: Central Bank Digital Currencies (CBDCs): The State Strikes Back

The advent of cryptocurrencies and decentralized finance has ushered in a wave of financial innovation that challenges traditional monetary systems. In response, central banks around the world have begun developing Central Bank Digital Currencies (CBDCs)—digital versions of their national currencies designed to combine the efficiency of digital payments with the stability of central bank backing. This chapter explores the mechanics, motivations, and implications of CBDCs, examining their potential to reshape global financial systems while addressing the societal and geopolitical challenges they pose.

The Rise of CBDCs: Why Now?

Central bank digital currencies are not a new concept, but their development has accelerated dramatically in recent years. This surge is driven by a convergence of factors:

The Decline of Cash:
As cash usage dwindles, particularly in developed economies, central banks face the risk of losing relevance in retail transactions. CBDCs offer a way for central banks to remain integral to everyday financial activity in a cashless world.

The Challenge of Cryptocurrencies:
The rise of Bitcoin, Ethereum, and other cryptocurrencies has highlighted the potential of decentralized systems to bypass traditional financial intermediaries. While cryptocurrencies remain volatile and speculative, their growing adoption has prompted central banks to develop alternatives that maintain institutional control while leveraging similar technological advances.

Technological Advancements:
Innovations in blockchain, distributed ledger technology (DLT), and secure digital infrastructure have made it feasible to implement CBDCs at scale. These technologies enable real-time settlement, improved transparency, and reduced costs for cross-border transactions.

Geopolitical Motivations:
The launch of China's digital yuan has amplified concerns among Western nations about the erosion of their monetary dominance. CBDCs are seen as a tool to preserve economic sovereignty and influence in an increasingly competitive global landscape.

How CBDCs Work: A Technological Overview

CBDCs differ from both cryptocurrencies and traditional digital payments in fundamental ways. Unlike cryptocurrencies, which operate on decentralized networks, CBDCs are issued and controlled by central banks. This centralized design ensures that CBDCs retain the stability and trust associated with fiat currencies.

CBDCs can be implemented in two main forms:

- **Retail CBDCs:** Designed for everyday use by the general public, retail CBDCs function as digital cash. They are accessed through digital wallets and can be used for payments, transfers, and savings.
- **Wholesale CBDCs:** These are intended for financial institutions and are used to settle interbank transactions. Wholesale CBDCs improve the efficiency and security of large-scale financial operations.

The underlying technology of CBDCs can vary. While some systems use blockchain or DLT, others rely on centralized databases. The choice of technology reflects a balance between security, scalability, and regulatory control.

The Promise of CBDCs

Proponents argue that CBDCs offer numerous benefits for consumers, businesses, and governments:

Financial Inclusion:
CBDCs can provide access to financial services for unbanked populations by eliminating the need for traditional bank accounts. In regions with limited banking infrastructure, digital wallets connected to CBDCs could democratize access to money.

Efficiency and Cost Reduction:
CBDCs streamline payment systems, reducing transaction costs and settlement times. For cross-border payments, CBDCs eliminate intermediaries, enabling near-instantaneous transfers with lower fees.

Monetary Policy Innovation:
CBDCs give central banks new tools for implementing monetary policy. For instance, programmable CBDCs could enable targeted stimulus payments, ensuring that funds are spent in specific sectors or within defined timeframes.

Combating Illicit Activity:
By creating an auditable trail for transactions, CBDCs can reduce tax evasion, money laundering, and other financial crimes. The transparency of CBDCs enhances regulatory oversight.

Challenges and Risks

While the potential benefits of CBDCs are significant, their implementation raises a host of challenges and risks:

Privacy Concerns:
The traceability of CBDC transactions raises alarms about surveillance and the erosion of financial privacy. Without robust safeguards, CBDCs could empower governments to monitor and control individual spending behavior.

Cybersecurity Threats:
The centralization of CBDCs creates single points of failure, making them attractive targets for cyberattacks. A successful attack on a CBDC system could destabilize entire economies.

Disruption to Banking Systems:
Widespread adoption of retail CBDCs could reduce the role of commercial banks in the financial ecosystem. If consumers shift deposits to CBDC accounts, banks may face funding shortages, undermining their ability to lend and invest.

Technical Complexity:
Designing and implementing a secure, scalable, and interoperable CBDC system is a daunting task. Central banks must navigate technological challenges while ensuring that CBDCs integrate seamlessly with existing financial infrastructure.

Global Case Studies

Several countries are at the forefront of CBDC development, offering valuable insights into their potential and pitfalls:

China:
The People's Bank of China (PBOC) launched pilot programs for the digital yuan in 2020, making it the most advanced CBDC initiative among major economies. The digital yuan is designed to enhance financial inclusion, reduce reliance on cash, and strengthen China's monetary sovereignty. However, critics argue that its centralized design exacerbates privacy concerns and extends state control.

Sweden:
The Riksbank's development of the e-krona reflects Sweden's leadership in cashless innovation. The e-krona aims to ensure public access to legal tender in an increasingly digital economy, while maintaining the stability of the Swedish financial system.

The European Union and the United States:
Both regions are in the exploratory phases of CBDC development. The European Central Bank (ECB) is evaluating the potential of a digital euro, focusing on privacy and resilience. In the US, the Federal Reserve has adopted a cautious approach, emphasizing research and stakeholder engagement.

Geopolitical Implications
CBDCs are not merely financial tools; they are instruments of geopolitical strategy. The digital yuan, for example, has sparked concerns about China's growing influence in global trade and finance. By offering an alternative to the US dollar in international transactions, the digital yuan could undermine the dollar's dominance as the world's reserve currency.

Conversely, Western nations view CBDCs as a means to counterbalance these developments and maintain their economic influence. The race to develop CBDCs has become a proxy for broader geopolitical competition, highlighting the intersection of technology, economics, and power.

Ethical and Philosophical Considerations

Beyond their technical and economic dimensions, CBDCs raise ethical questions about the role of money in society. Should governments have the ability to program currency, dictating how and when it can be spent? How do we balance the benefits of transparency with the need for individual autonomy?

These questions underscore the broader societal implications of CBDCs. As central banks chart the future of money, they must navigate a delicate balance between innovation and ethics, ensuring that the systems they create serve the public good.

Conclusion: The State Strikes Back

CBDCs represent a pivotal moment in the evolution of money, offering the potential to revolutionize financial systems while reinforcing the authority of central banks. However, their success will depend on how governments address the challenges of privacy, security, and inclusion. As nations race to develop their own digital currencies, the world is witnessing the reassertion of state control in an era defined by decentralization. The next chapters will explore how these dynamics interact with the broader forces shaping the future of money.

Chapter 4: Decentralized Finance (DeFi): A Revolution or a Bubble?

The advent of decentralized finance, or DeFi, represents one of the most significant financial innovations of the 21st century. Built on blockchain technology, DeFi eliminates traditional financial intermediaries, enabling peer-to-peer transactions, lending, borrowing, and investment. Proponents argue that it democratizes access to financial services, while critics warn of volatility, risks, and speculative excesses. As billions of dollars flow into DeFi platforms, the question remains: is DeFi a transformative force or an unsustainable bubble?

The Foundations of Decentralized Finance

Decentralized finance is an ecosystem of financial applications built on blockchain networks, primarily Ethereum. By utilizing smart contracts—self-executing agreements encoded directly into the blockchain—DeFi platforms facilitate complex financial transactions without the need for banks, brokers, or other intermediaries. This disintermediation offers reduced costs, faster transactions, and greater transparency.

DeFi encompasses a broad range of applications:

- Decentralized exchanges (DEXs): Platforms like Uniswap and SushiSwap enable users to trade cryptocurrencies directly with one another, bypassing centralized exchanges.
- Lending and borrowing protocols: Services such as Aave and Compound allow users to lend assets to earn interest or borrow funds by collateralizing cryptocurrencies.
- Yield farming: Participants earn rewards by providing liquidity to DeFi protocols, a process akin to earning interest in traditional finance but with higher risks and returns.
- Stablecoins: Cryptocurrencies like DAI are pegged to fiat currencies, offering stability in an otherwise volatile market.

Unlike traditional finance, where transactions are verified and controlled by central authorities, DeFi transactions are governed by code. This open-source nature allows for innovation and customization but also introduces risks related to security and regulatory oversight.

The Promise of DeFi: A Financial Revolution

Advocates of decentralized finance see it as a revolutionary force that addresses many of the inefficiencies and inequities of traditional finance. The key promises of DeFi include:

Financial Inclusion:
DeFi removes barriers to entry, allowing anyone with an internet connection to access financial services. This democratization is particularly impactful in regions with underdeveloped banking infrastructure, where traditional financial systems exclude large portions of the population.

Transparency and Trust:
Blockchain's immutable ledger provides an unprecedented level of transparency. All transactions are recorded publicly, reducing the potential for fraud and corruption. Trust is transferred from institutions to code.

Innovation and Efficiency:
DeFi accelerates financial innovation by enabling developers to create interoperable applications. These "money Legos" allow for the rapid development of new financial instruments, reducing costs and increasing accessibility.

The decentralized nature of DeFi also reduces systemic risks associated with centralized intermediaries. During financial crises, traditional institutions can become points of failure, as seen in the 2008 global financial collapse. DeFi's distributed architecture minimizes such vulnerabilities.

Risks and Challenges

Despite its potential, DeFi faces significant hurdles that could undermine its promise:

Volatility and Speculation:
DeFi markets are notoriously volatile, driven by speculative investments in nascent projects. The rapid rise and fall of token prices can lead to massive losses for participants, deterring wider adoption.

Security Vulnerabilities:
The reliance on smart contracts introduces unique risks. Bugs or vulnerabilities in the code can be exploited, leading to losses of millions of dollars. High-profile attacks, such as the $600 million Poly Network hack in 2021, highlight the fragility of the ecosystem.

Regulatory Uncertainty:
DeFi exists in a legal gray area. Governments and regulators are grappling with how to classify and oversee decentralized platforms. Striking a balance between innovation and compliance is a challenge that could shape the future of the industry.

Accessibility and Usability:
While DeFi aims to promote inclusion, its technical complexity often creates barriers for non-technical users. Navigating wallets, exchanges, and protocols can be daunting for newcomers, limiting widespread adoption.

Liquidity Risks:
Yield farming and liquidity pools attract users with the promise of high returns, but these systems are susceptible to market fluctuations and liquidity crises. The collapse of a major protocol could trigger cascading failures across the ecosystem.

Global Perspectives and Case Studies

The growth of DeFi has been uneven across regions, reflecting differences in infrastructure, regulation, and adoption:

North America and Europe:
These regions dominate DeFi activity, with significant investment from institutional and retail participants. However, regulatory scrutiny is intensifying, with governments seeking to impose anti-money laundering (AML) and know-your-customer (KYC) requirements on DeFi platforms.

Developing Economies:
In countries like Nigeria and Argentina, DeFi offers an alternative to unstable currencies and restrictive banking systems. Stablecoins, in particular, provide a hedge against inflation and economic instability.

Asia:
Asia has emerged as a hub for blockchain innovation, with countries like Singapore fostering DeFi ecosystems through supportive regulatory frameworks. However, China's crackdown on cryptocurrencies underscores the delicate balance between innovation and control.

DeFi: Revolution or Bubble?

DeFi's meteoric rise has drawn comparisons to previous financial bubbles, from the dot-com boom of the 1990s to the ICO frenzy of 2017. Skeptics argue that DeFi's rapid growth is unsustainable, driven by speculative greed rather than genuine utility. However, proponents counter that the underlying technology represents a paradigm shift, with applications that extend far beyond speculative trading.

Whether DeFi evolves into a lasting financial system or fades into obscurity depends on its ability to address key challenges. Improving security, enhancing user experience, and navigating regulatory landscapes will be critical to its long-term success.

Philosophical Implications

DeFi raises profound questions about the nature of trust and the role of intermediaries in society. Traditional finance is built on institutional trust —banks, governments, and regulatory bodies serve as guarantors of stability. DeFi replaces this trust with code, decentralizing power and creating new opportunities for innovation.

Yet, the erosion of intermediaries also shifts responsibility to individuals. Users must navigate complex systems, secure their own assets, and assess the risks of participating in an unregulated market. This shift challenges traditional notions of accountability and raises ethical questions about the distribution of risk and reward.

Conclusion: The Road Ahead

DeFi stands at a crossroads. Its potential to democratize finance and foster innovation is undeniable, but so are the risks it poses. As the ecosystem matures, the balance between revolution and regulation will determine its trajectory. Will DeFi usher in a new era of financial freedom, or will it collapse under the weight of its own ambitions? The answer lies in the collective actions of developers, regulators, and participants.

The next chapter will explore another transformative force in the financial landscape: artificial intelligence, and how it is reshaping financial decision-making at every level.

Chapter 5: Artificial Intelligence and Financial Decision-Making

Artificial intelligence (AI) has become a transformative force in finance, reshaping how decisions are made at every level, from individual consumers to institutional investors. AI's ability to process vast datasets, identify patterns, and make predictions with unprecedented speed and accuracy has unlocked new opportunities while introducing complex challenges. As the financial ecosystem becomes increasingly data-driven, AI is not merely a tool but a defining characteristic of modern financial systems.

This chapter explores how AI is revolutionizing financial decision-making, examining its applications, benefits, and risks. From algorithmic trading to credit scoring, AI-driven systems are altering the dynamics of finance in ways that demand both excitement and caution.

The Role of AI in Financial Decision-Making

At its core, AI leverages machine learning, natural language processing, and predictive analytics to analyze data and make informed decisions. These capabilities are applied across various financial domains:

Investment Management:
AI-driven platforms analyze market data to develop optimized investment strategies. Robo-advisors, such as Betterment and Wealthfront, offer personalized portfolio recommendations based on user inputs, democratizing access to professional-grade financial advice.

Algorithmic Trading:
High-frequency trading (HFT) firms use AI algorithms to execute trades at lightning speeds, exploiting market inefficiencies to maximize profits. These algorithms can analyze historical data, predict price movements, and execute trades in milliseconds.

Credit Scoring and Lending:
Traditional credit scoring models rely on limited datasets, often excluding unbanked or underbanked populations. AI expands the scope of credit assessment by analyzing alternative data sources, such as utility payments and social media activity, providing a more nuanced picture of creditworthiness.

Fraud Detection and Risk Management:
AI systems monitor transactions in real time to detect anomalies and potential fraud. By identifying suspicious patterns, such as unusual spending behavior or account access from unexpected locations, AI enhances security and minimizes financial losses.

Case Studies: AI in Action

AI's transformative potential is evident in several high-profile applications:

Bridgewater Associates:
One of the world's largest hedge funds, Bridgewater uses AI to develop trading algorithms that mimic human decision-making processes. By simulating various economic scenarios, these algorithms help the firm navigate market volatility.

Ant Group:
The Chinese fintech giant employs AI to assess credit risk for its lending services, using data from Alibaba's e-commerce platform. This approach has enabled Ant to extend credit to millions of small businesses and individuals who lack traditional credit histories.

JP Morgan Chase:
AI-powered tools like COiN (Contract Intelligence) automate the review of legal documents, reducing the time required to analyze contracts and improving accuracy. This application highlights AI's potential to streamline operational processes in finance.

The Benefits of AI in Finance

The adoption of AI in finance offers numerous advantages, transforming traditional practices into dynamic, efficient processes:

Enhanced Accuracy and Speed:
AI systems can process and analyze data at scales far beyond human capability, enabling faster and more accurate decision-making. This advantage is particularly evident in trading, where milliseconds can mean millions of dollars.

Personalization:
By analyzing user data, AI tailors financial products and services to individual needs. This personalization improves customer satisfaction and broadens access to financial tools.

Cost Efficiency:
Automation reduces the need for manual processes, lowering operational costs for financial institutions. Robo-advisors, for instance, offer investment management services at a fraction of the cost of human advisors.

Inclusivity:
AI-driven credit scoring models extend financial services to underbanked populations, fostering inclusion and economic empowerment.

Risks and Ethical Concerns

Despite its benefits, AI introduces risks and ethical dilemmas that must be carefully managed:

Bias and Discrimination:
AI algorithms are only as unbiased as the data they are trained on. Historical biases in lending or hiring practices can be perpetuated, leading to discriminatory outcomes. For example, a credit scoring model might unfairly penalize individuals from disadvantaged backgrounds if it relies on biased datasets.

Opacity and Accountability:
The complexity of AI systems often renders their decision-making processes opaque, a phenomenon known as the "black box" problem. This lack of transparency raises questions about accountability when AI-driven decisions go wrong.

Market Volatility:
The use of AI in trading can exacerbate market volatility. During the 2010 Flash Crash, for example, algorithmic trading systems triggered a rapid sell-off, wiping out $1 trillion in market value within minutes.

Cybersecurity Threats:
As financial institutions become increasingly reliant on AI, they also become more vulnerable to cyberattacks. Hackers targeting AI systems can exploit weaknesses in algorithms, potentially causing widespread disruptions.

Regulatory Challenges

Governments and regulatory bodies face the daunting task of overseeing AI in finance. Striking a balance between fostering innovation and protecting consumers is no small feat. Key areas of concern include:

Data Privacy:
The use of personal data in AI systems must comply with privacy regulations, such as the General Data Protection Regulation (**GDPR**) in the European Union.

Algorithmic Accountability:
Regulators are exploring ways to ensure that AI algorithms are transparent, fair, and auditable. Initiatives such as explainable AI (XAI) aim to make machine learning models more interpretable.

Global Coordination:
As AI systems operate across borders, international cooperation is essential to establish consistent regulatory standards and prevent regulatory arbitrage.

The Future of AI in Finance

The integration of AI into financial systems is still in its early stages, but its trajectory points toward deeper and more pervasive adoption. Emerging trends include:

Autonomous Financial Agents:
AI systems capable of executing financial decisions independently, from managing investments to negotiating contracts, are on the horizon.

Quantum Computing:
The convergence of AI and quantum computing promises breakthroughs in risk modeling, portfolio optimization, and encryption, but also introduces new risks to data security.

Ethical AI:
The development of ethical frameworks for AI in finance will be critical to addressing concerns about bias, transparency, and accountability.

Philosophical Considerations

AI's influence on financial decision-making extends beyond economics. It raises profound questions about the nature of trust, the role of human agency, and the ethics of delegating critical decisions to machines. As AI systems become more sophisticated, society must grapple with what it means to rely on algorithms for decisions that were once the domain of human judgment.

Conclusion: A Double-Edged Sword

AI represents a double-edged sword in finance, offering unparalleled efficiency and innovation while introducing risks that demand careful oversight. Its potential to democratize access to financial services and optimize decision-making is undeniable, but its long-term impact will depend on how society addresses its challenges. The next chapter will delve into the intersection of financial inequality and technological change, exploring how these dynamics shape the distribution of wealth in a rapidly evolving world.

Chapter 6: Global Inequality and the Future of Wealth Distribution

The Promise and Perils of Financial Innovation

The rise of new financial technologies and systems has the potential to revolutionize the global economy, but it also risks exacerbating existing inequalities. While blockchain, artificial intelligence, and decentralized finance are celebrated for their democratizing potential, they remain predominantly accessible to those with the knowledge, resources, and infrastructure to leverage them. As wealth continues to concentrate in fewer hands, the question arises: will technological innovation bridge the gap or widen the divide?

The distribution of global wealth has always been uneven, but recent decades have seen a stark acceleration in inequality. According to the 2024 Global Wealth Report, the richest 1% of individuals now control over 46% of global wealth, while the bottom 50% account for less than 2%. This disparity is not merely a product of economic systems; it is a reflection of systemic barriers, policy decisions, and historical injustices. Economic globalization and technological advancements have played dual roles in shaping this landscape. On the one hand, they have created immense wealth and lifted millions out of poverty, particularly in emerging economies. On the other, they have concentrated power and resources among a small elite, perpetuating cycles of inequality.

The Role of Technology in Widening or Bridging the Divide

Technology has the power to both democratize and concentrate wealth, depending on how it is implemented and accessed. In theory, innovations such as blockchain, artificial intelligence, and digital finance can empower marginalized communities by providing access to tools and opportunities previously reserved for the privileged. However, the reality is often more complex.

Access to new financial technologies remains uneven. Rural populations, low-income households, and individuals in developing countries often lack the digital infrastructure, financial literacy, or resources needed to participate in the digital economy. For example, while decentralized finance platforms promise financial inclusion, they are primarily used by tech-savvy investors in developed markets.

The rapid growth of cryptocurrency markets has created a new class of digital millionaires and billionaires. However, studies show that cryptocurrency ownership is highly concentrated, with a small percentage of wallets controlling the majority of assets. This mirrors the inequalities seen in traditional financial systems. Furthermore, artificial intelligence and automation are transforming industries, increasing productivity and reducing costs. Yet, they also threaten to displace millions of workers, particularly in sectors such as manufacturing, logistics, and customer service. This displacement disproportionately affects low- and middle-income workers, further widening the wealth gap.

Global Contexts: Uneven Impacts of Technological Change

The impact of technological innovation on inequality can be seen in various contexts. Mobile money platforms such as M-Pesa have revolutionized access to financial services in countries like Kenya, allowing unbanked populations to save, transfer, and invest money. However, the benefits have been unevenly distributed, with urban populations and wealthier individuals gaining the most. In countries like Argentina and Venezuela, cryptocurrencies have provided a lifeline for citizens grappling with hyperinflation and currency devaluation. Yet, the majority of crypto activity remains speculative, benefiting those with the resources and knowledge to invest.

Meanwhile, in the United States and Europe, automation has created new industries and opportunities while displacing traditional jobs.

Governments have struggled to implement policies that retrain workers and distribute the benefits of technological progress equitably. The uneven adoption and application of these innovations highlight the challenges of ensuring that technological progress benefits all.

Policy Solutions for a More Inclusive Future

Addressing global inequality in the context of technological change requires proactive and inclusive policy measures. Expanding internet access, particularly in rural and underserved areas, is essential for enabling participation in the digital economy. Governments and private sector partnerships can play a critical role in bridging the digital divide. Financial literacy programs are crucial for empowering individuals to navigate new financial technologies. Initiatives that target marginalized communities can help ensure that innovation benefits everyone, not just the privileged few.

Wealth taxes, corporate taxation, and other redistributive policies can mitigate the concentration of wealth. Revenues from these measures can be reinvested in education, healthcare, and infrastructure to promote equity. Additionally, as automation threatens traditional employment, universal basic income (UBI) has gained traction as a potential solution for reducing inequality. By providing a guaranteed income to all citizens, UBI could offer a safety net in an era of rapid technological change.

Ethical Questions and Societal Priorities

Beyond economic considerations, inequality raises profound ethical questions about fairness, justice, and human dignity. In a world where resources are finite, how do we ensure that technological progress benefits everyone? What responsibility do innovators, investors, and policymakers have in addressing systemic inequities? The concentration of wealth is not merely an economic issue; it reflects societal values and priorities. By examining the structural forces that perpetuate inequality, we can begin to envision a more equitable future.

Conclusion: Charting a Path Forward

Global inequality remains one of the defining challenges of our time, and its interplay with financial innovation adds layers of complexity. While technology offers tools for addressing systemic barriers, it also has the potential to exacerbate disparities if left unchecked. Building a more inclusive financial future requires collective action, ethical considerations, and policies that prioritize equity alongside growth. The next chapter will delve into the rise of green finance and the growing demand for sustainable investment, exploring how financial systems can align with environmental and social priorities.

Chapter 7: Green Finance and the Push for Sustainability

The Rise of Green Finance

As the world grapples with the escalating impacts of climate change, the financial sector has emerged as a pivotal player in driving sustainability. Green finance—the integration of environmental, social, and governance (ESG) criteria into financial decision-making—is rapidly transforming how capital is allocated, influencing everything from investment strategies to corporate accountability. With trillions of dollars flowing into ESG-aligned assets, green finance represents a fundamental shift in the priorities of global markets.

The origins of green finance can be traced back to the late 20th century, when ethical investing began gaining traction among socially conscious investors. However, the concept has evolved significantly, driven by the urgent need to address climate risks and align economic activities with global sustainability goals such as the Paris Agreement. Today, green finance encompasses a broad spectrum of initiatives, including green bonds, sustainable funds, and climate-focused investment strategies. These instruments aim to channel resources toward projects that mitigate environmental harm, promote renewable energy, and foster social equity.

Instruments of Green Finance

Green bonds, a cornerstone of sustainable finance, are debt securities issued to fund environmentally friendly projects. Since their inception in 2007, the green bond market has grown exponentially, reaching over $1 trillion in issuance by 2023. Governments, corporations, and multilateral institutions use these bonds to finance initiatives such as renewable energy installations, energy-efficient infrastructure, and sustainable agriculture. The European Union, for instance, has issued billions in green bonds as part of its Green Deal, aiming to achieve carbon neutrality by 2050.

Sustainable funds, another critical component, focus on investing in companies that meet ESG criteria. These funds evaluate potential investments based on factors such as carbon footprint, labor practices, and corporate governance. With the rise of passive investing, ESG-focused exchange-traded funds (ETFs) have become increasingly popular, allowing retail investors to align their portfolios with their values. However, concerns about "greenwashing"—the practice of exaggerating or falsifying sustainability claims—highlight the need for standardized metrics and rigorous oversight.

Another innovative tool is carbon trading, which allows companies to buy and sell carbon credits to offset their emissions. While this market incentivizes emissions reductions, critics argue that it can also enable companies to continue polluting by purchasing credits rather than reducing their carbon footprint. Nonetheless, carbon markets are expanding, with regions like the European Union and California implementing robust cap-and-trade systems.

The Impact of Green Finance

The adoption of green finance has profound implications for the global economy. It has redefined risk assessment by incorporating climate-related risks into financial models. Banks and insurance companies now evaluate clients and projects not only on financial metrics but also on their environmental impact. This shift reflects a growing recognition that climate risks—from extreme weather events to regulatory changes—can have material consequences for financial stability.

Green finance also drives innovation by channeling capital into emerging technologies. Investments in renewable energy, electric vehicles, and energy storage have accelerated the transition to a low-carbon economy. For example, advances in battery technology, supported by green financing, have made renewable energy more viable by addressing the intermittency of solar and wind power.

Similarly, sustainable agriculture initiatives funded by green loans have introduced precision farming techniques that optimize resource use and reduce environmental degradation.

On a societal level, green finance fosters greater accountability and transparency among corporations. ESG reporting frameworks, such as those developed by the Global Reporting Initiative (GRI) and the Task Force on Climate-related Financial Disclosures (TCFD), require companies to disclose their environmental impact, creating pressure to adopt sustainable practices. This trend has empowered stakeholders, from investors to consumers, to demand greater responsibility from businesses.

Challenges and Criticisms

Despite its promise, green finance faces significant challenges. One of the most pressing issues is the lack of standardized definitions and metrics for sustainability. What qualifies as a "green" project varies widely, leading to inconsistencies and confusion among investors. Efforts to address this issue, such as the EU's Taxonomy for Sustainable Activities, aim to provide clear criteria, but global harmonization remains elusive.

Another concern is greenwashing, which undermines the credibility of sustainable finance. Some companies and funds exaggerate their environmental commitments to attract investment, eroding trust and misallocating capital. Addressing this issue requires robust regulatory frameworks and third-party verification to ensure the authenticity of ESG claims.

The accessibility of green finance also raises questions. While developed countries have the resources to implement ambitious sustainability initiatives, many developing nations lack the financial infrastructure and capital to participate fully in the green economy. Bridging this gap will require international cooperation, including mechanisms such as climate finance pledges from wealthy nations to support sustainable development in the Global South.

Finally, there is the challenge of balancing short-term profitability with long-term sustainability. Investors often prioritize immediate returns, creating tension with the longer time horizons needed for environmental projects to yield benefits. Overcoming this challenge will require a cultural shift in investment priorities and stronger incentives for sustainable practices.

The Future of Green Finance

The future of green finance lies in its integration into mainstream financial systems. As awareness of climate risks grows, sustainability will increasingly influence every aspect of financial decision-making, from retail banking to global capital markets. Technological advancements, such as blockchain, could enhance transparency and efficiency in green finance by enabling real-time tracking of sustainability metrics. For instance, blockchain-based platforms could verify the authenticity of carbon credits or ensure that green bond proceeds are used as intended.

Moreover, public-private partnerships will play a critical role in scaling green finance. Governments can provide incentives, such as tax breaks and subsidies, to encourage private investment in sustainable initiatives. Collaboration between financial institutions, technology companies, and non-governmental organizations can also accelerate innovation and expand access to green finance.

Educational initiatives will be crucial in fostering a sustainability mindset among investors and the general public. By promoting financial literacy and raising awareness of green finance options, stakeholders can drive demand for sustainable products and hold institutions accountable.

Conclusion: Aligning Finance with a Sustainable Future

Green finance represents a transformative approach to addressing the interconnected challenges of economic growth and environmental sustainability.

By redirecting capital flows toward projects that prioritize the health of the planet and the well-being of its people, it offers the potential to create a more equitable and resilient global economy. Achieving this vision, however, requires overcoming substantial hurdles, including the standardization of sustainability metrics and ensuring equitable access for developing nations.

The evolution of green finance has already begun to reshape the financial sector, from influencing investment strategies to redefining corporate accountability. As these systems mature, they must balance innovation with inclusivity, ensuring that developing countries and marginalized communities can benefit equally from sustainable practices. Mechanisms such as global climate finance agreements and targeted subsidies can play a pivotal role in bridging this gap.

Moreover, the future success of green finance lies in the collective efforts of all stakeholders. Governments must implement policies that incentivize sustainable practices, businesses must integrate ESG principles into their core operations, and individuals must advocate for accountability and transparency in financial markets. By fostering a collaborative approach, green finance can become a catalyst for global change, driving the transition to a low-carbon, socially equitable economy.

As we look ahead, green finance will undoubtedly remain a central pillar in the pursuit of sustainability. Its integration into mainstream financial systems promises to align economic activities with ecological stewardship, creating a framework that benefits both present and future generations. By embracing innovation, fostering partnerships, and ensuring ethical oversight, we can harness the full potential of green finance to build a brighter, greener future for all.

Chapter 8: The Tokenized Economy: Beyond Currency

The Emergence of Tokenization

Tokenization, the process of converting rights or ownership of an asset into a digital token on a blockchain, represents a groundbreaking shift in how value is created, exchanged, and managed. While initially associated with cryptocurrencies, tokenization has evolved far beyond digital currencies to encompass a wide range of assets, including real estate, art, intellectual property, and even personal income streams. By enabling fractional ownership and seamless transferability, tokenization is poised to democratize access to wealth and redefine the dynamics of global financial markets.

The concept of tokenization stems from the principles of blockchain technology, which ensures transparency, security, and immutability. A token can represent virtually anything of value, serving as a digital representation of tangible or intangible assets. These tokens are traded on decentralized platforms, bypassing traditional intermediaries and reducing transaction costs. The tokenized economy's potential lies in its ability to unlock liquidity, reduce barriers to entry, and create new investment opportunities for individuals and institutions alike.

Tokenization in Practice

The practical applications of tokenization are vast and transformative. One of the most prominent examples is the tokenization of real estate. Traditionally, investing in property required substantial capital and often involved lengthy legal processes. Tokenization simplifies this by allowing investors to purchase fractional ownership in a property through digital tokens, making real estate investment more accessible. Platforms such as RealT and Brickblock have pioneered this approach, enabling individuals to invest in properties with minimal capital.

Art and collectibles are another sector benefiting from tokenization. Non-fungible tokens (NFTs) have revolutionized the art world by creating digital certificates of authenticity for artwork, enabling artists to sell directly to buyers without intermediaries. The success of platforms like OpenSea and Rarible demonstrates the growing appetite for tokenized art, with some NFTs selling for millions of dollars.

Tokenization also extends to intellectual property, allowing creators to monetize their work in innovative ways. Musicians, for instance, can tokenize future royalties from their music, giving fans the opportunity to invest in and share in their success. Similarly, entrepreneurs can tokenize equity in their startups, raising funds from a global pool of investors without traditional venture capital constraints.

The Benefits of Tokenization

The tokenized economy offers numerous advantages, reshaping traditional finance and expanding access to investment opportunities. One of the most significant benefits is increased liquidity. Assets that were once considered illiquid, such as real estate or fine art, can now be traded on digital platforms, unlocking value and enabling faster transactions. This liquidity democratizes investment by allowing individuals to buy and sell fractional ownership, lowering the barriers to entry for smaller investors.

Tokenization also enhances transparency and security. Blockchain technology ensures that all transactions are recorded on an immutable ledger, reducing the risk of fraud and enhancing trust among participants. Smart contracts—self-executing agreements encoded on the blockchain—streamline processes by automating tasks such as dividend distribution or compliance checks.

Another critical benefit is inclusivity. By fractionalizing assets, tokenization allows individuals to invest in high-value assets with minimal capital. This democratization opens up opportunities for underrepresented groups and fosters greater participation in the global economy. Additionally, the global nature of blockchain networks enables cross-border transactions without the complexities of traditional financial systems.

Challenges and Risks

Despite its promise, the tokenized economy faces significant challenges. Regulatory uncertainty is one of the most pressing issues. Governments and regulatory bodies are still grappling with how to classify and oversee tokenized assets. The lack of standardized frameworks creates confusion for issuers and investors, potentially stifling innovation.

Security vulnerabilities are another concern. While blockchain technology is inherently secure, the platforms and applications built on top of it can be susceptible to hacks and cyberattacks. High-profile incidents, such as the $600 million Poly Network hack, underscore the importance of robust security measures.

Scalability also poses a challenge. As tokenization platforms grow, they must handle increasing transaction volumes without compromising efficiency or user experience. Current blockchain networks, such as Ethereum, often face congestion and high transaction fees, which can deter adoption.

Furthermore, the speculative nature of token markets raises concerns about volatility and market manipulation. The rapid rise and fall of token prices can lead to significant financial losses for investors, particularly those who lack experience in navigating volatile markets.

Ethical and Philosophical Implications

The tokenized economy raises profound ethical and philosophical questions about ownership, value, and access. While tokenization has the potential to democratize wealth, it also risks perpetuating existing inequalities if access to platforms and resources remains uneven. The question of who controls the infrastructure of tokenization—and how that control is wielded—is central to its future.

Moreover, tokenization challenges traditional notions of value. By creating digital representations of intangible assets, it blurs the line between physical and virtual economies. This shift forces society to reconsider what constitutes "real" wealth and how it should be distributed.

The Road Ahead

The tokenized economy is still in its infancy, but its potential to reshape global finance is undeniable. As regulatory frameworks mature and technological innovations address scalability and security challenges, tokenization is likely to become an integral part of mainstream financial systems. Collaboration between governments, private sector players, and blockchain developers will be crucial in building a robust and inclusive ecosystem.

Public awareness and education will also play a pivotal role. As more individuals and institutions understand the benefits and risks of tokenization, they can make informed decisions and contribute to the growth of the tokenized economy. By fostering transparency, inclusivity, and ethical practices, the tokenized economy can fulfill its promise of democratizing wealth and expanding opportunities for all.

Conclusion: A Paradigm Shift in Value Creation

The tokenized economy represents a paradigm shift in how value is created, exchanged, and managed. By leveraging blockchain technology, it has the potential to democratize access to wealth, enhance transparency, and foster innovation across industries. However, realizing this vision requires addressing significant challenges, from regulatory uncertainty to technological limitations.

As the world transitions toward a more digital and interconnected economy, tokenization offers a glimpse into a future where ownership is more accessible, markets are more efficient, and opportunities are more inclusive. By navigating the complexities of this emerging landscape with care and foresight, we can harness the transformative power of the tokenized economy to create a more equitable and prosperous global financial system.

Chapter 9: Hyperinflation and the Risks of a Digital-Only World

Introduction: Hyperinflation in Historical Context

Hyperinflation, characterized by an uncontrollable and accelerating increase in prices, has historically been one of the most destabilizing economic phenomena. Its catastrophic effects on economies, societies, and governments are well-documented, from Weimar Germany's infamous currency collapse in the 1920s to Zimbabwe's trillion-dollar banknotes in the early 21st century. These historical examples illustrate the devastating consequences of hyperinflation: the erosion of savings, the collapse of financial institutions, and widespread social unrest.

As the global economy moves toward an increasingly digital monetary system, the potential risks of hyperinflation take on new dimensions. Digital currencies—whether decentralized cryptocurrencies like Bitcoin or centralized Central Bank Digital Currencies (CBDCs)—introduce opportunities for innovation but also raise critical questions about monetary stability. What happens when the safeguards of traditional financial systems are removed? How do digital-only systems influence the potential for hyperinflation, and are we prepared to mitigate these risks?

Digital Economies: Opportunities and Vulnerabilities

The transition to digital currencies offers numerous benefits, including efficiency, transparency, and financial inclusion. However, it also introduces unique vulnerabilities that could exacerbate the risk of hyperinflation. One such vulnerability lies in the potential for unchecked money creation. In traditional systems, central banks regulate the supply of money through monetary policy tools such as interest rates and open market operations. Digital currencies, particularly those issued by central banks, could make it easier to expand the money supply with the click of a button.

Moreover, the speed and scale of digital transactions amplify the impact of monetary policy decisions. In a digital-only world, central banks can inject liquidity into the economy almost instantaneously. While this capability is useful in times of crisis, such as during the COVID-19 pandemic, it also increases the risk of overcorrection, where excessive money supply floods the economy, devaluing the currency and triggering inflationary spirals.

Cryptocurrencies add another layer of complexity. Unlike fiat currencies, which are backed by governments, cryptocurrencies derive their value from market demand and perceived scarcity. If trust in a cryptocurrency erodes, its value can plummet overnight, causing chaos in economies reliant on these assets. Conversely, speculative bubbles in crypto markets can lead to asset price inflation, destabilizing broader financial systems.

Case Studies: Lessons from History and Modern Experiments

The historical examples of hyperinflation offer valuable lessons for navigating the risks of a digital-only world. During the Weimar Republic, excessive printing of fiat currency to pay reparations led to hyperinflation, eroding public trust in money and the government. A similar dynamic could occur in a digital context if central banks overuse their ability to issue digital currencies without adequate oversight or accountability.

Zimbabwe's hyperinflation in the 2000s underscores the dangers of monetary mismanagement. The government's decision to print money to finance public spending resulted in inflation rates that rendered the national currency worthless. In a digital economy, such policies could be implemented even more rapidly, magnifying their effects.

Modern experiments with digital currencies provide a glimpse into potential future risks and benefits. El Salvador's adoption of Bitcoin as legal tender, for instance, has sparked debates about the stability of cryptocurrencies in national economies.

While proponents argue that Bitcoin's fixed supply protects against inflation, critics highlight its extreme volatility and limited acceptance as barriers to effective monetary policy.

The Role of Central Bank Digital Currencies (CBDCs)

CBDCs represent a middle ground between fiat currencies and decentralized cryptocurrencies, offering the benefits of digital money while retaining government oversight. However, their implementation must be carefully managed to avoid inflationary risks. Central banks must establish clear rules for money creation and distribution, ensuring that digital currencies do not undermine existing monetary frameworks.

One proposed solution is to tie CBDC issuance to tangible assets or economic performance metrics, creating a built-in mechanism to prevent overissuance. Additionally, integrating programmable features into CBDCs, such as expiration dates for stimulus payments, could help control money velocity and mitigate inflationary pressures. However, these innovations also raise ethical questions about the extent of government control over individual financial behavior.

Mitigating Hyperinflation in a Digital World

Addressing the risks of hyperinflation in a digital economy requires a multi-faceted approach. Regulatory frameworks must be updated to account for the unique characteristics of digital currencies, ensuring that central banks maintain control over monetary policy while allowing for innovation. International coordination will be critical, as digital currencies operate across borders and are influenced by global market dynamics.

Technological safeguards are equally important. Blockchain technology offers transparency and traceability, enabling real-time monitoring of money supply and transactions. These features can enhance oversight and reduce the likelihood of policy missteps.

However, reliance on technology also introduces vulnerabilities, such as cyberattacks and system failures, which must be addressed through robust cybersecurity measures.

Public trust will play a pivotal role in preventing hyperinflation. In a digital-only world, trust in the stability and value of money will depend on the perceived competence and integrity of monetary authorities. Transparent communication, consistent policy implementation, and mechanisms for public accountability will be essential in maintaining this trust.

Ethical and Social Considerations

The shift to a digital-only economy raises ethical and social questions about the distribution of risk and responsibility. Hyperinflation disproportionately affects vulnerable populations, eroding savings and reducing purchasing power for those least able to adapt. Policymakers must prioritize inclusivity and equity in designing digital monetary systems, ensuring that safeguards protect the most at-risk groups.

Moreover, the potential for hyperinflation highlights the broader societal implications of digital money. If financial systems become too reliant on technology, what happens in the event of a systemic failure? How do we balance the need for innovation with the risks of overreach? These questions underscore the importance of a cautious and measured approach to digital transformation.

Conclusion: Navigating the Risks

As the global economy embraces digital currencies, the potential for hyperinflation represents a critical challenge that must be addressed with foresight and diligence. While digital money offers unprecedented opportunities for efficiency and inclusion, it also introduces risks that could destabilize economies if not carefully managed.

By learning from history, implementing robust regulatory and technological safeguards, and fostering public trust, we can navigate these risks and build a resilient and equitable digital monetary system.

The next chapter will explore another transformative aspect of the financial landscape: the interplay between ethics and technology, examining how innovation challenges our understanding of value, trust, and accountability in the financial world.

Chapter 10: The Philosophy of Money: Value Beyond Economics

Introduction: Rethinking the Foundations of Money

Money is often reduced to its practical functions as a medium of exchange, a store of value, and a unit of account. However, these definitions fail to capture the profound philosophical and cultural dimensions of money. Beyond its economic utility, money embodies social agreements, power structures, and ethical considerations that shape human relationships and societal values. As technology transforms the nature of money, it becomes imperative to revisit its philosophical underpinnings to understand how these changes influence not only economies but also the fabric of human existence.

From the emergence of barter systems to the rise of digital currencies, money has always been more than a tool for commerce; it is a manifestation of collective trust and shared belief. Its evolution mirrors humanity's shifting priorities, from survival and trade to innovation and interconnectedness. This chapter explores money's deeper meanings, its impact on society, and how emerging financial technologies challenge our understanding of value, trust, and morality.

The Social Construct of Money

At its core, money is a social construct—a shared belief system that assigns value to otherwise inert objects or concepts. Historically, items such as shells, beads, and precious metals gained monetary status not because of intrinsic value but because societies collectively agreed on their worth. This agreement is the foundation of all monetary systems, from ancient coinage to modern fiat currencies and cryptocurrencies.

Fiat money, for instance, relies entirely on trust in the issuing authority. Without this trust, paper notes and digital balances lose their meaning.

Similarly, cryptocurrencies like Bitcoin derive their value from the belief in blockchain technology and the consensus of decentralized networks. The philosophical implications of this are profound: money is only as real as the trust and belief that sustain it.

This constructivist view of money highlights its role as a tool for organizing society. It enables cooperation on a massive scale, from local markets to global trade networks. Yet, it also reinforces power dynamics, as those who control monetary systems wield significant influence over economies and societies. The emergence of decentralized finance and blockchain technologies seeks to democratize this control, raising questions about the future balance of power.

The Moral and Ethical Dimensions of Money

Money has always been intertwined with morality and ethics, shaping societal norms and individual behavior. Philosophers from Aristotle to Karl Marx have grappled with the ethical implications of wealth, inequality, and commerce. In today's world, these debates are more relevant than ever as financial technologies redefine the boundaries of ownership, access, and accountability.

One critical ethical question concerns the distribution of wealth. The growing concentration of resources among a small elite contrasts sharply with the promises of economic democratization often associated with digital finance. Blockchain, for instance, offers tools for inclusion but also risks perpetuating inequalities if access to technology and financial literacy remains uneven.

The concept of ethical investing further illustrates the moral dimensions of money. The rise of ESG (Environmental, Social, and Governance) criteria reflects a growing demand for financial systems that prioritize sustainability and social responsibility. However, challenges such as greenwashing and conflicting priorities complicate the pursuit of ethical financial practices.

The Role of Trust in Financial Systems

Trust is the cornerstone of all monetary systems. It underpins the value of currencies, the functioning of financial institutions, and the stability of economies. Without trust, markets collapse, and commerce ceases. Yet, trust is not static; it evolves with cultural, technological, and political changes.

The transition to digital and decentralized financial systems is reshaping the dynamics of trust. Traditional systems rely on centralized authorities such as governments and banks to guarantee the value and security of money. In contrast, blockchain-based systems distribute trust across networks, relying on transparency and cryptographic security rather than institutional authority.

This shift raises philosophical questions about the nature of trust itself. Can algorithms and code replace human institutions as arbiters of trust? What happens when technology fails or is manipulated? These questions highlight the need for a nuanced understanding of trust in the age of digital money.

Redefining Value in the Digital Age

As money evolves, so does the concept of value. Traditional notions of value are rooted in scarcity, utility, and labor. Gold, for example, is valuable because it is rare, durable, and historically regarded as a universal medium of exchange. Fiat currencies derive value from their role in facilitating economic activity and their backing by governments.

Digital currencies and tokenized assets challenge these traditional notions. NFTs (non-fungible tokens), for instance, assign value to digital art and collectibles based on perceived uniqueness and cultural significance rather than physical properties. Cryptocurrencies like Bitcoin redefine scarcity through algorithmic design, creating digital assets with fixed supplies.

This redefinition of value has cultural and philosophical implications. It shifts the emphasis from material wealth to symbolic and experiential wealth, reflecting changes in societal priorities. However, it also raises questions about the sustainability and ethical implications of digital value creation. Are we merely replicating the speculative excesses of traditional finance in a new medium, or are we forging a more inclusive and equitable system?

The Interplay Between Money and Identity

Money is not only an economic tool but also a marker of identity. It reflects personal values, cultural affiliations, and social status. The choices individuals make about how to earn, spend, and invest money reveal their priorities and beliefs.

In the digital age, this interplay between money and identity takes on new dimensions. Cryptocurrencies and decentralized finance empower individuals to express their values through financial decisions, whether by supporting blockchain projects aligned with their ideals or investing in tokenized assets that resonate with their identities. At the same time, the anonymity and pseudonymity enabled by digital currencies challenge traditional notions of financial accountability and transparency.

This duality raises ethical and practical questions. How do we balance the freedom of financial expression with the need for accountability? What role should financial systems play in shaping individual and collective identities?

Conclusion: Money as a Reflection of Humanity

The philosophy of money extends far beyond economics, encompassing profound questions about trust, value, ethics, and identity. It serves not only as a practical tool but as a mirror reflecting the complexities of human relationships and societal structures.

As financial technologies reshape the nature of money, they compel us to reconsider our fundamental understanding of what it means to value, to trust, and to share resources in a globalized and increasingly digitized world.

By examining money through a philosophical lens, we uncover its dual role as both a connector and a divider. It unites people through shared systems of trust and belief, enabling vast networks of cooperation, but it also reveals the fault lines of inequality, power imbalances, and systemic exclusion. The evolution of money, from ancient bartering systems to blockchain and cryptocurrencies, is not merely a technical or economic process; it is a cultural and ethical journey that encapsulates humanity's collective struggles, aspirations, and innovations.

As the world embraces new forms of money, we must remain mindful of its deeper dimensions. Emerging financial technologies, while transformative, carry risks of perpetuating existing inequalities or creating new ones. They challenge us to think critically about the distribution of wealth, the role of institutions, and the moral implications of financial systems designed for profit. These systems must strive to balance efficiency with equity, innovation with inclusion, and growth with sustainability.

Ultimately, the future of money will depend on our collective ability to align its evolution with the principles of human flourishing. By fostering open dialogue, interdisciplinary collaboration, and ethical considerations, we can ensure that financial innovation contributes not only to economic advancement but also to a more just, compassionate, and resilient society. Money, at its core, is a reflection of humanity—its values, its ambitions, and its potential. As we navigate the uncharted waters of the future, this reflection must inspire us to build systems that honor the dignity and interconnectedness of all people.

By 2025, more individuals will opt for food that is not only good for their health but also the planet, reducing environmental impact while improving overall well-being.

How You Can Prepare:
- Start learning about personalized nutrition options, such as DNA testing or gut microbiome analysis, to tailor your diet to your specific needs.
- Choose plant-based or sustainable foods that reduce your carbon footprint and support healthier living.
- Experiment with meal planning to ensure you're getting balanced nutrition that aligns with your health goals.

Conclusion: Holistic Health for a Future-Ready You

By 2025, the future of health will be more holistic, personalized, and tech-driven. From AI-powered fitness and digital healthcare to personalized nutrition and mental well-being, it's clear that taking care of your health will require a more integrated and proactive approach. Start preparing now by adopting healthy habits, embracing new technologies, and ensuring that both your physical and mental health are prioritized for the long haul.

In the next chapter, we'll explore how to stay motivated and resilient in the face of change, ensuring that you're not just surviving but thriving in 2025 and beyond.

Chapter 11: Financial Inclusion in the Age of Technology

Introduction: Bridging the Global Divide

Financial inclusion—the ability for individuals and businesses to access affordable financial products and services—is a cornerstone of economic development and social equity. Despite decades of progress, billions of people worldwide remain excluded from formal financial systems, unable to access banking, credit, or insurance. This exclusion perpetuates poverty, limits economic opportunity, and exacerbates inequality.

The rise of digital technology presents a unique opportunity to bridge this divide. Mobile banking, blockchain, decentralized finance (DeFi), and artificial intelligence (AI) have begun to transform how financial services are delivered, particularly in underserved regions. Yet, these innovations also pose challenges, from technological barriers to regulatory complexities. This chapter explores the promises and pitfalls of using technology to achieve financial inclusion, highlighting case studies, emerging trends, and critical considerations for the future.

The Current State of Financial Exclusion

According to the World Bank's 2023 Global Findex Database, approximately 1.4 billion adults worldwide remain unbanked. The majority live in low- and middle-income countries, particularly in sub-Saharan Africa, South Asia, and Latin America. Women, rural populations, and marginalized groups are disproportionately affected by financial exclusion, facing systemic barriers such as lack of identification, inadequate infrastructure, and limited financial literacy.

The consequences of exclusion are profound. Without access to credit, entrepreneurs struggle to grow their businesses. Without savings accounts, families cannot build financial resilience.

Without insurance, individuals are left vulnerable to economic shocks such as illness or natural disasters. Addressing these gaps is essential for fostering inclusive economic growth and reducing global inequality.

How Technology is Expanding Access

Technology has begun to redefine the landscape of financial inclusion by reducing costs, increasing accessibility, and enabling innovative solutions. Mobile banking is perhaps the most transformative example. Platforms like M-Pesa in Kenya and GCash in the Philippines have revolutionized financial access by allowing users to send, receive, and save money using basic mobile phones. These services bypass the need for traditional banking infrastructure, reaching populations in remote and underserved areas.

Blockchain and DeFi offer additional avenues for inclusion. By eliminating intermediaries, these technologies reduce transaction costs and increase transparency. For instance, cross-border remittances—a lifeline for millions of families—can be processed more efficiently using blockchain-based platforms like Ripple. DeFi protocols, such as Aave and Compound, enable individuals to access loans and earn interest on savings without requiring a credit history or bank account.

Artificial intelligence is also playing a critical role. AI-powered platforms can analyze alternative data sources, such as mobile phone usage or social media activity, to assess creditworthiness. This approach has enabled financial institutions to extend credit to individuals who lack traditional credit histories, particularly in emerging markets. Additionally, AI-driven chatbots and apps are improving financial literacy by providing personalized advice and education.

Case Studies: Successes and Challenges

The transformative potential of technology is evident in several real-world examples:

- **M-Pesa (Kenya):** Since its launch in 2007, M-Pesa has grown to serve over 50 million users across Africa, providing services such as savings accounts, microloans, and bill payments. Studies show that M-Pesa has lifted hundreds of thousands of households out of poverty by enabling financial independence and entrepreneurship.

- **Stellar (Global):** The Stellar blockchain facilitates cross-border payments with low fees, enabling migrants to send remittances to their families without the high costs associated with traditional money transfer services. This has increased disposable income for recipient families, improving their quality of life.

- **India's Aadhaar Program:** The world's largest biometric identification system has enabled millions of Indians to access banking and government subsidies. Coupled with the Pradhan Mantri Jan Dhan Yojana financial inclusion initiative, Aadhaar has significantly increased the percentage of banked adults in India.

However, challenges remain. Digital divides persist, with millions lacking the internet access or digital literacy needed to use these technologies. Additionally, the reliance on digital platforms raises concerns about data privacy and cybersecurity. For instance, breaches in biometric systems like Aadhaar could compromise the sensitive personal information of millions.

Barriers to Digital Financial Inclusion

While technology has the potential to democratize access, several barriers hinder its full realization:

- Infrastructure Gaps: In many developing countries, unreliable electricity, limited internet connectivity, and lack of smartphone penetration restrict access to digital financial services.

- Regulatory Hurdles: Governments often struggle to regulate emerging technologies, leading to uncertainty that discourages investment and innovation. Balancing innovation with consumer protection remains a significant challenge.

- Financial Literacy: Many individuals lack the knowledge or confidence to navigate digital financial platforms. Without targeted education initiatives, these populations risk being left behind.

- Gender Disparities: Women face unique barriers to financial inclusion, including cultural norms, limited access to identification, and restricted mobility. Addressing these disparities is essential for achieving universal inclusion.

The Role of Policy and Collaboration

Achieving financial inclusion requires coordinated efforts among governments, private sector players, and non-governmental organizations (NGOs). Policymakers must create enabling environments that encourage innovation while safeguarding consumer rights. Examples include India's regulatory sandbox for fintech startups and Kenya's supportive policies for mobile money providers.

Public-private partnerships can amplify impact. For instance, collaborations between telecom companies and banks have driven the success of mobile banking in Africa. NGOs and international organizations can also play a pivotal role by funding pilot projects, providing technical assistance, and advocating for inclusive policies.

International cooperation will also be critical. Global organizations like the United Nations and the World Bank must work alongside local governments to provide funding and expertise for large-scale financial inclusion initiatives. Cross-border collaborations can address common challenges, such as regulatory disparities and interoperability between financial systems.

Emerging Technologies and Future Trends

The future of financial inclusion lies in leveraging emerging technologies to address existing gaps while anticipating new challenges. Blockchain's potential for secure, decentralized identity systems could help address the issue of undocumented individuals, enabling them to access financial services. These systems can provide tamper-proof digital identities that are portable across borders, simplifying verification processes for refugees and migrants.

AI-driven platforms will continue to refine credit assessments, expanding access to loans and insurance. Machine learning models trained on diverse data sources can predict creditworthiness with remarkable accuracy, reducing the reliance on traditional credit scoring methods. Additionally, AI-powered tools can offer tailored financial advice, helping users make informed decisions and avoid predatory practices.

Digital currencies, including central bank digital currencies (CBDCs), could further enhance inclusion by providing a government-backed alternative to cash. However, their implementation must be carefully managed to avoid excluding populations without access to digital infrastructure. Ensuring interoperability between digital currencies and traditional systems will be critical. Governments could also consider implementing offline functionality for digital wallets to reach communities with limited internet access.

Education will play a pivotal role in ensuring the success of these initiatives. Financial literacy programs must be integrated into broader efforts to promote digital inclusion, equipping individuals with the skills and confidence needed to navigate complex financial systems. Gamified learning tools and localized content can make education more engaging and relevant to diverse audiences.

Conclusion: Building an Inclusive Financial Ecosystem

Financial inclusion is both a moral imperative and an economic necessity. By leveraging technology, we can create systems that empower individuals, reduce poverty, and foster sustainable development. However, this vision will only be realized if we address the barriers that hinder access, from infrastructure gaps to regulatory complexities.

Collaboration, innovation, and education will be key. Governments must invest in digital infrastructure and enact supportive policies. Private sector players must design user-friendly platforms that prioritize accessibility and security. NGOs and international organizations must continue to advocate for and fund initiatives that promote inclusion.

Ultimately, financial inclusion is about more than access; it is about opportunity, dignity, and equality. By harnessing the transformative power of technology, we can build a financial ecosystem that leaves no one behind. In doing so, we pave the way for a more equitable and prosperous future for all—one where financial systems work for everyone, regardless of geography, gender, or socioeconomic status.

Chapter 12: Ethics and Innovation in Financial Systems

Introduction: Balancing Progress with Responsibility

As financial systems evolve, propelled by technological advancements and globalization, the ethical dimensions of innovation become increasingly critical. Financial technologies, from blockchain and artificial intelligence to digital currencies, offer transformative possibilities but also present moral dilemmas. How do we ensure that these innovations benefit all members of society and do not exacerbate existing inequalities? How do we strike a balance between efficiency and accountability, profit and sustainability?

This chapter delves into the ethical considerations surrounding modern financial systems. By exploring historical contexts, current practices, and future implications, it provides a framework for understanding how innovation and ethics intersect in the ever-changing landscape of global finance.

Historical Perspectives: Ethics in Financial Systems

Ethical considerations in finance are not new. From the principles of fair trade in ancient commerce to the emergence of socially responsible investing in the 20th century, societies have long grappled with the moral implications of financial practices. Key historical moments illustrate the tension between profit and ethics:

- The Medici Banking Era (15th Century): The Medici family's banking empire in Renaissance Italy exemplified the duality of financial power. While their innovations in credit and banking fueled economic growth, they also faced accusations of corruption and exploitation, highlighting the ethical responsibilities of financial leaders.

- The 2008 Global Financial Crisis: This crisis exposed systemic failures in accountability and transparency, as reckless lending and speculative investments led to economic devastation for millions. The aftermath saw renewed calls for ethical reform, emphasizing the need for greater oversight and fairness in financial systems.

These historical lessons underscore the importance of embedding ethics into financial innovation, ensuring that technological advancements align with societal values.

Current Ethical Challenges in Financial Technology

Modern financial technologies present unique ethical challenges that demand careful consideration:

- **Data Privacy and Security:** As digital finance relies on vast amounts of data, concerns about privacy and cybersecurity are paramount. Unauthorized data collection, breaches, and surveillance threaten individual rights and erode trust in financial institutions. Ethical finance must address these risks by implementing robust data protection measures, ensuring that individuals retain control over their personal information, and adhering to stringent privacy regulations like GDPR.

- **Algorithmic Bias:** AI-driven financial systems, such as credit scoring algorithms and trading bots, can inadvertently perpetuate biases present in their training data. For instance, algorithms trained on historical financial data might unfairly disadvantage marginalized groups. Addressing algorithmic bias requires transparency in AI design, regular audits to identify discriminatory patterns, and inclusive datasets that reflect diverse populations.

- **Exclusion and Accessibility:** While digital finance promises inclusion, its reliance on technology can exclude those without access to digital infrastructure or literacy. For example, rural communities or older populations may struggle to adopt mobile banking or blockchain solutions. Ethical innovation must prioritize accessibility by developing user-friendly interfaces, investing in digital infrastructure for underserved areas, and offering educational programs to build digital literacy.

- **Environmental Impact:** The environmental footprint of financial technologies, particularly blockchain and cryptocurrency mining, raises ethical questions about sustainability. Bitcoin mining, for example, consumes as much energy as some small countries, contributing to carbon emissions. Solutions include transitioning to energy-efficient consensus mechanisms, such as proof-of-stake, and integrating renewable energy sources into mining operations.

The Role of Regulation and Governance

Ethical innovation in finance requires robust regulation and governance. Governments, international organizations, and industry leaders must collaborate to establish frameworks that prioritize transparency, accountability, and inclusivity. Key areas for action include:

- **Standardizing Ethical Practices:** Developing global standards for ethical financial practices, such as ESG (Environmental, Social, and Governance) criteria, can ensure consistency and accountability across industries. These standards provide a benchmark for assessing corporate behavior, encouraging firms to adopt sustainable practices and disclose their social and environmental impacts.

- **Promoting Inclusive Policies:** Policies that prioritize financial inclusion, such as subsidies for digital infrastructure in underserved areas or education programs to enhance financial literacy, can reduce disparities. Governments can collaborate with private entities to create financial products tailored to the needs of marginalized communities, ensuring that no one is left behind.

- **Enhancing Oversight:** Regulatory bodies must adapt to the rapid pace of technological change, addressing risks such as algorithmic bias, market manipulation, and data misuse. This includes establishing independent oversight committees to monitor compliance with ethical standards and introducing penalties for violations.

- **Fostering Collaboration:** Public-private partnerships and international cooperation can amplify efforts to embed ethics in financial systems, leveraging diverse perspectives and resources. Collaborative initiatives, such as the United Nations' Principles for Responsible Investment, encourage stakeholders to align their strategies with global sustainability goals.

Emerging Trends and Future Implications

Several trends are shaping the future of ethical innovation in finance:

- **Decentralized Governance Models:** Blockchain technology enables decentralized decision-making, reducing reliance on centralized authorities. For instance, decentralized autonomous organizations (DAOs) allow stakeholders to vote on key decisions, promoting transparency and accountability. However, decentralized systems also face challenges, such as ensuring equitable participation and preventing governance capture by powerful entities.

- Ethical AI: Advances in AI ethics, such as explainable AI and fairness-focused algorithms, are addressing concerns about bias and accountability. For example, financial institutions are adopting AI tools that can provide transparent explanations for decisions, such as why a loan application was approved or denied, fostering trust among users.

- Sustainability Initiatives: The rise of green finance and sustainable investing reflects a growing recognition of environmental and social responsibilities. Asset managers are increasingly incorporating ESG factors into their investment decisions, while green bonds finance projects that combat climate change. These initiatives demonstrate how profit motives can align with broader societal goals.

- Digital Identity Systems: Secure, decentralized identity solutions can empower individuals by giving them control over their personal data. Blockchain-based digital identities enable seamless access to financial services while protecting user privacy. For example, refugees can use digital identities to access banking services without traditional documentation, fostering financial inclusion.

The Ethical Imperative: A Call to Action

The ethical challenges and opportunities in modern financial systems demand a proactive and collaborative approach. Financial institutions, policymakers, technologists, and consumers all have roles to play in shaping a more equitable and sustainable future. Specific actions include:

- **Embedding Ethics in Design:** Developers of financial technologies must prioritize ethical considerations from the outset, incorporating principles such as fairness, transparency, and inclusivity into their designs. This involves conducting impact assessments during the development phase and engaging diverse stakeholders to identify potential risks and benefits.

- Empowering Consumers: Financial literacy programs and accessible tools can help consumers make informed decisions, holding institutions accountable for their practices. Governments and NGOs can collaborate to deliver targeted educational campaigns, ensuring that individuals understand their rights and responsibilities in digital financial systems.

- Advocating for Change: Civil society organizations and thought leaders can drive conversations about ethical finance, advocating for policies and practices that align with societal values. Public advocacy can influence corporate behavior, encouraging firms to prioritize ethical considerations in their operations.

Conclusion: Innovation with Integrity

As financial systems continue to evolve, the intersection of ethics and innovation becomes increasingly significant. By addressing the moral dimensions of technological progress, we can ensure that financial systems serve not only economic efficiency but also human dignity and societal well-being.

Innovation must be guided by integrity, balancing the pursuit of progress with a commitment to fairness, sustainability, and inclusion. Financial systems have the power to shape societies, influence cultures, and impact the daily lives of billions. This immense responsibility requires a collective effort to embed ethical considerations at every stage of innovation, from initial design to implementation and scaling.

The journey toward ethical financial systems begins with fostering open dialogue among diverse stakeholders. Policymakers, technologists, corporations, and civil society must collaborate to address pressing challenges such as data privacy, environmental sustainability, and equitable access. This dialogue should be informed by historical lessons and grounded in a forward-looking vision that prioritizes inclusivity and resilience.

Collaboration is essential to building trust in financial systems. Public-private partnerships can accelerate progress by pooling resources and expertise, while international cooperation can establish consistent standards and prevent regulatory arbitrage. For instance, aligning global efforts to regulate decentralized technologies can ensure that innovation does not outpace oversight, reducing risks to consumers and economies.

At the individual level, empowering consumers through education and accessible tools is paramount. Financial literacy initiatives should go beyond basic knowledge to address the complexities of modern financial systems, equipping individuals to navigate AI-driven platforms, digital currencies, and decentralized networks confidently. An informed public can drive demand for ethical practices and hold institutions accountable for their decisions.

Moreover, integrating ethical considerations into the core values of financial institutions can lead to transformative change. By embracing principles such as transparency, accountability, and social responsibility, organizations can build systems that not only generate profits but also contribute to broader societal goals. This alignment of profit motives with ethical imperatives represents the future of sustainable finance.

As we look ahead, the challenges and opportunities of financial innovation will continue to evolve. Emerging technologies such as quantum computing, advanced AI, and next-generation blockchains will bring new possibilities and risks. To navigate these changes, we must remain steadfast in our commitment to ethical principles, ensuring that technological advancements uplift humanity rather than deepen divides.
The path to ethical innovation is not without obstacles, but it is one worth pursuing. By fostering collaboration, prioritizing education, and maintaining a steadfast commitment to integrity, we can create financial systems that reflect our highest aspirations. These systems have the potential to empower individuals, reduce inequalities, and pave the way for a future where technology serves as a force for good, leaving no one behind.

Chapter 13: The Intersection of Globalization and Financial Systems

Introduction: A World Without Borders?

Globalization, the increasing interconnectedness of economies, cultures, and societies, has profoundly reshaped financial systems over the past century. The advent of technology has accelerated this process, enabling capital to flow across borders with unprecedented speed and efficiency. However, globalization has also introduced complexities and challenges that require careful navigation. From financial crises that ripple across continents to the growing influence of multinational corporations, the interplay between globalization and financial systems has transformed the way we think about money, markets, and governance.

This chapter explores the multifaceted relationship between globalization and finance, examining its historical roots, current dynamics, and future implications. By delving into key case studies and emerging trends, it provides a comprehensive understanding of how globalization is shaping the financial systems of tomorrow.

Historical Evolution: The Globalization of Finance

The globalization of financial systems is not a new phenomenon. Its roots can be traced back to the early days of international trade and commerce:

- **The Silk Road (2nd Century BCE – 14th Century):** This ancient trade network connected East Asia, the Middle East, and Europe, facilitating the exchange of goods, currencies, and ideas. It laid the groundwork for global financial systems by introducing cross-border trade and the use of diverse currencies.

- **The Gold Standard (19th – Early 20th Century):** The adoption of the gold standard provided a unified basis for international trade, linking currencies to a fixed amount of gold. While it promoted stability, it also made economies vulnerable to external shocks and rigid monetary policies.

- **The Bretton Woods System (1944 – 1971):** Established after World War II, this system pegged major currencies to the US dollar, which was convertible to gold. It fostered global economic growth but collapsed under the strain of inflation and trade imbalances.

These milestones illustrate the evolving nature of globalization in finance, highlighting both its benefits and its challenges.

Key Dynamics in the Globalized Financial System

In today's interconnected world, financial systems are shaped by several key dynamics:

- **Capital Flows:** The liberalization of financial markets has enabled capital to move freely across borders, fueling economic growth and investment. However, it has also increased volatility, as seen in the 1997 Asian financial crisis and the 2008 global financial crisis. These crises underscore the need for robust regulatory frameworks to manage capital flows.

- **Multinational Corporations (MNCs):** MNCs play a pivotal role in the global economy, driving investment, innovation, and job creation. Yet, their influence raises concerns about corporate accountability, tax avoidance, and economic sovereignty. The ability of MNCs to shift profits to low-tax jurisdictions highlights the need for international cooperation on taxation and governance.

- **Digital Finance:** The rise of fintech and digital currencies has transformed global finance, enabling seamless cross-border transactions and expanding access to financial services. Platforms like PayPal and Wise facilitate international money transfers at lower costs, while blockchain technology offers secure and transparent alternatives to traditional banking.

- **Economic Inequality:** Globalization has widened the gap between rich and poor, both within and between countries. While some regions have benefited from increased trade and investment, others have been left behind. Addressing these disparities requires targeted policies that promote inclusive growth and equitable access to resources.

Case Studies: Globalization in Action

Several examples illustrate the complex interplay between globalization and financial systems:

- **The European Union (EU):** The EU's single market and shared currency (the euro) demonstrate the potential of regional integration. By eliminating trade barriers and harmonizing regulations, the EU has fostered economic growth and stability. However, the 2008 debt crisis exposed the vulnerabilities of shared monetary policies without fiscal union, prompting reforms to strengthen economic governance.

- **China's Belt and Road Initiative (BRI):** This ambitious infrastructure project aims to connect Asia, Africa, and Europe through a network of trade routes and investment. While the BRI has spurred economic development in participating countries, it has also raised concerns about debt sustainability and geopolitical influence.

- **Cryptocurrency Adoption in Developing Economies:** Countries like El Salvador and Nigeria are leveraging cryptocurrencies to address economic challenges, such as inflation and limited access to banking. While these initiatives highlight the potential of digital finance, they also underscore the risks of volatility and regulatory uncertainty.

Challenges and Risks of Globalized Finance

Globalization offers significant opportunities but also introduces risks that require careful management. One notable aspect is the disparity in how globalization impacts different economies. Developed nations often reap the majority of the benefits due to their established infrastructures, robust financial systems, and greater access to capital. In contrast, developing economies face unique challenges, including dependency on foreign investment and vulnerability to external shocks. For instance, countries heavily reliant on exports are disproportionately affected by global market fluctuations, which can destabilize local industries and hinder long-term growth.

- **Systemic Risk:** The interconnectedness of financial systems means that crises in one region can quickly spread to others. For example, the 2008 global financial crisis originated in the US housing market but had far-reaching impacts on economies worldwide.

- **Regulatory Fragmentation:** Differences in regulatory frameworks across countries create challenges for managing cross-border activities. Harmonizing regulations is essential for reducing risks and ensuring fair competition.

- **Cultural and Political Resistance:** Globalization often faces backlash from those who feel left behind or threatened by foreign influence. Populist movements and trade protectionism highlight the need for policies that address the social and cultural dimensions of globalization.

- **Environmental Impact:** The globalization of finance has fueled industrial growth and resource extraction, contributing to environmental degradation. Sustainable finance initiatives, such as green bonds and ESG investing, aim to align economic activities with environmental goals.

The Future of Globalized Financial Systems

The future of globalization in finance will be shaped by several emerging trends:

- **Digital Currencies and CBDCs:** Central bank digital currencies (CBDCs) have the potential to enhance cross-border payments and reduce reliance on traditional banking systems. However, their implementation must balance innovation with privacy and security concerns.

- **Decentralized Finance (DeFi):** DeFi platforms are challenging traditional financial intermediaries by offering peer-to-peer services. While they promote financial inclusion, they also pose regulatory and security risks.

- **Geopolitical Shifts:** The rise of emerging economies, such as China and India, is reshaping the global financial landscape. These shifts will influence the balance of power and the development of international financial norms.

- **Climate Finance:** Addressing climate change will require significant investment in sustainable infrastructure and technologies. Global financial systems must mobilize resources to support these efforts while ensuring equitable access for developing countries.

Conclusion: Navigating a Globalized Future

Globalization has transformed financial systems, creating opportunities for growth and innovation while introducing new risks and challenges. The interconnectivity of today's world demands not only economic integration but also cultural sensitivity and a shared commitment to equitable progress. Policymakers, businesses, and individuals alike must recognize that globalization is not a one-size-fits-all process; it requires nuanced approaches tailored to the needs of diverse populations.

As we navigate this complex landscape, collaboration and adaptability will be essential for building a resilient and inclusive global economy. International institutions such as the IMF and World Bank must lead efforts to harmonize regulations and provide support to economies struggling with globalization's challenges. At the same time, financial institutions must innovate responsibly, ensuring that their practices promote transparency and foster trust.

Communities also have a pivotal role to play. By advocating for ethical policies and sustainable practices, individuals can influence the trajectory of globalization to better reflect shared human values. Moreover, technological advancements such as blockchain and AI offer tools to mitigate some of globalization's inherent risks, providing secure, efficient, and equitable solutions for cross-border financial interactions.

The intersection of globalization and finance is a dynamic and evolving frontier. By fostering dialogue, collaboration, and ethical decision-making, we can harness the potential of globalized financial systems to create a more equitable and sustainable future for all. In doing so, we must remain vigilant to ensure that the benefits of globalization are broadly shared, leaving no one behind in the pursuit of progress.

Policymakers must work together to harmonize regulations, promote sustainable practices, and address systemic risks. Financial institutions must embrace innovation while prioritizing accountability and transparency. Individuals and communities must advocate for policies that reflect their values and protect their interests.

The intersection of globalization and finance is a dynamic and evolving frontier. By fostering dialogue, collaboration, and ethical decision-making, we can harness the potential of globalized financial systems to create a more equitable and sustainable future for all.

Chapter 14: The Role of Trust in the Future of Financial Systems

Introduction: Trust as the Cornerstone of Finance

Trust is the foundation upon which all financial systems are built. It underpins the value of money, the stability of markets, and the functioning of financial institutions. Without trust, the intricate web of transactions, contracts, and investments that drive economies would unravel. In an era of rapid technological advancements and increasing globalization, the nature of trust in financial systems is undergoing profound changes.

This chapter explores the evolving role of trust in finance, examining its historical roots, current challenges, and future implications. By analyzing case studies and emerging trends, it highlights the critical importance of fostering trust in a rapidly changing financial landscape.

Historical Perspectives: Trust in Traditional Financial Systems

The concept of trust in finance has evolved alongside the development of monetary systems and institutions. Over centuries, financial trust has been built, challenged, and redefined:

- **The Rise of Banking:** In medieval Europe, the establishment of banks introduced a new layer of trust, allowing individuals and businesses to deposit money and access credit. Banking families like the Medicis became symbols of financial reliability, even as they navigated the ethical complexities of their era. Trust in these institutions was rooted in their ability to safeguard assets and provide liquidity in times of need.

- **The Gold Standard:** The gold standard, which linked currencies to physical gold reserves, provided a tangible basis for trust in monetary systems. This system created a sense of security as it limited the arbitrary expansion of money supply. However, it also constrained monetary flexibility, making economies vulnerable to deflation and external shocks.

- **The Post-War Era:** Following World War II, institutions like the International Monetary Fund (IMF) and the World Bank were created to promote global economic stability. These organizations relied on mutual trust among nations to foster cooperation and prevent financial crises. Their ability to mediate and provide resources in times of economic distress established a foundation for global economic governance.

These historical examples underscore the centrality of trust in maintaining financial stability and facilitating economic growth, demonstrating that trust evolves alongside societal needs and technological capabilities.

Modern Challenges to Financial Trust

In today's interconnected world, trust in financial systems faces significant challenges, each requiring nuanced solutions:

- **Financial Crises:** Events like the 2008 global financial crisis have eroded trust in traditional financial institutions. The collapse of major banks and widespread economic fallout highlighted systemic weaknesses and raised questions about accountability and oversight. The crisis revealed how opaque financial instruments and poor risk management could undermine global stability.

- **Technological Disruption:** The rise of digital finance, blockchain, and artificial intelligence has introduced new paradigms of trust. While these technologies offer transparency and efficiency, they also challenge traditional notions of trust by decentralizing authority and relying on algorithms and code. This shift raises questions about who bears responsibility when these systems fail.

- **Fraud and Cybersecurity:** As financial systems become increasingly digital, they are more vulnerable to fraud, hacking, and data breaches. High-profile incidents, such as the Equifax breach and cryptocurrency exchange hacks, have shaken public confidence in digital platforms. Effective cybersecurity measures and accountability mechanisms are essential to rebuild trust.

- **Misinformation and Scams:** The proliferation of misinformation and financial scams on social media and other digital platforms has further undermined trust. Individuals are often targeted by fraudulent schemes, highlighting the need for education and robust regulatory frameworks. Public awareness campaigns and clear penalties for fraudsters are necessary to protect vulnerable populations.

Building Trust in Digital Financial Systems

The transition to digital and decentralized financial systems requires new approaches to building and maintaining trust. Several strategies are crucial:

- **Transparency:** Blockchain technology offers a potential solution by providing transparent and immutable records of transactions. By making financial activities traceable, blockchain can reduce fraud and enhance accountability. For example, smart contracts automatically enforce agreements, reducing reliance on intermediaries.

- **Regulatory Oversight:** Governments and international organizations must establish clear regulatory frameworks for digital finance. These frameworks should address issues such as consumer protection, data privacy, and market manipulation. Transparent regulations can create an environment where innovation flourishes without compromising trust.

- **Security Measures:** Strengthening cybersecurity protocols is essential to safeguarding digital financial systems. Innovations such as biometric authentication, multi-factor security, and decentralized identity solutions can enhance trust in digital platforms. These measures protect users from unauthorized access and ensure data integrity.

- **Education and Awareness:** Promoting financial literacy and digital awareness can empower individuals to make informed decisions and recognize potential risks. Public campaigns and educational initiatives should target vulnerable populations to reduce susceptibility to scams and fraud. Tailored programs for different demographics can ensure widespread understanding of digital finance.

The Role of Central Bank Digital Currencies (CBDCs)

CBDCs represent a significant innovation with the potential to reshape trust in financial systems. As government-backed digital currencies, CBDCs combine the advantages of digital finance with the stability and reliability of traditional fiat currencies. However, their implementation raises critical questions about trust:

- **Privacy vs. Transparency:** While CBDCs can enhance transparency in financial transactions, they also raise concerns about privacy. Striking the right balance between these priorities is essential to maintaining public trust. Transparent policies regarding data usage and strong encryption measures can address these concerns.

- **Interoperability:** Ensuring that CBDCs are interoperable with existing financial systems and other digital currencies will be crucial to their success. Collaborative efforts among central banks and financial institutions can build confidence in these new systems by reducing complexity and enhancing user experiences.

- **Accessibility:** CBDCs must be designed to promote financial inclusion, ensuring that all individuals, regardless of their technological capabilities or socioeconomic status, can access and benefit from digital currencies. Offline functionality and user-friendly interfaces can extend their reach to underserved populations.

Case Studies: Trust in Action

Several examples illustrate the importance of trust in modern financial systems:

- **Bitcoin and Blockchain:** Bitcoin's decentralized nature and transparent ledger have made it a symbol of trustless transactions. However, its association with volatility and illicit activities has limited its mainstream adoption, highlighting the complexities of building trust in decentralized systems. Regulatory clarity and educational efforts can help bridge these gaps.

- **The European Central Bank (ECB):** The ECB's response to the eurozone debt crisis demonstrates the role of central banks in restoring trust. By implementing measures such as quantitative easing and stricter fiscal rules, the ECB stabilized markets and regained public confidence. These actions underscore the importance of decisive and transparent policymaking.

- **India's Unified Payments Interface (UPI):** UPI's success in promoting digital payments in India reflects the importance of user-friendly platforms and government support in building trust. By enabling seamless transactions and fostering public-private collaboration, UPI has enhanced financial inclusion and trust in digital systems. Its model serves as a blueprint for other countries seeking to modernize payment systems.

The Future of Trust in Finance

As financial systems continue to evolve, trust will remain a fundamental pillar. Emerging trends that will shape the future of trust include:

- **Decentralized Autonomous Organizations (DAOs):** DAOs use blockchain technology to enable collective decision-making without centralized leadership. While they offer new models of governance, their success depends on building trust among participants and ensuring transparency. Mechanisms for dispute resolution and accountability are critical for their longevity.

- **Artificial Intelligence (AI):** AI-driven financial systems must prioritize ethical design and transparency to foster trust. Explainable AI, which provides clear insights into decision-making processes, can enhance confidence in AI-driven platforms. Continuous monitoring and unbiased training data are essential for maintaining credibility.

- **Global Cooperation:** Addressing global financial challenges, such as climate change and economic inequality, requires coordinated efforts. International cooperation can strengthen trust by promoting stability and equitable development. Collaborative initiatives, such as green finance programs, demonstrate how shared goals can build trust across borders.

Conclusion: Trust as the Foundation of Progress

Trust is the bedrock of financial systems, enabling economic growth, innovation, and social cohesion. As we navigate the complexities of a rapidly changing financial landscape, fostering trust requires a holistic approach that combines transparency, accountability, and collaboration.
The future of trust in finance depends on our ability to adapt to new technologies while preserving the principles that underpin economic stability. By embracing innovation with integrity and prioritizing the needs of all stakeholders, we can build financial systems that inspire confidence and empower individuals and communities worldwide.

Trust is not a static concept; it evolves with societal values, technological advancements, and economic realities. By fostering open dialogue, addressing emerging challenges, and maintaining a steadfast commitment to ethical principles, we can ensure that trust remains a cornerstone of financial progress, guiding us toward a more inclusive and resilient global economy. Through this commitment, financial systems can become not only efficient but also equitable, fostering a future where trust is not a luxury but a universal standard.

Chapter 15: Financial Resilience in an Era of Uncertainty

Introduction: The Need for Resilience

In an increasingly complex and unpredictable world, financial resilience has emerged as a critical concept for individuals, institutions, and economies. The ability to withstand and recover from economic shocks, market volatility, and global crises defines the sustainability and stability of financial systems. From the COVID-19 pandemic to geopolitical tensions and environmental challenges, recent events have highlighted the vulnerabilities of interconnected financial systems and the need for robust resilience strategies.

This chapter examines the principles and practices of financial resilience, exploring how stakeholders can adapt to uncertainty and foster stability. By analyzing historical precedents, current trends, and future innovations, it offers a roadmap for building financial systems capable of navigating an unpredictable future.

Historical Lessons on Resilience

Financial resilience has been tested and shaped by numerous historical events:

- **The Great Depression (1929–1939):** The collapse of global markets during the Great Depression underscored the importance of regulatory oversight and social safety nets. In its aftermath, measures such as the creation of the U.S. Federal Deposit Insurance Corporation (FDIC) and the New Deal programs were implemented to restore confidence and economic stability.

- **The 2008 Global Financial Crisis:** Triggered by the collapse of subprime mortgage markets, the crisis exposed systemic weaknesses in financial systems, from excessive risk-taking to inadequate oversight. Governments and central banks responded with coordinated interventions, including bailouts and quantitative easing, to stabilize markets and prevent further economic collapse.

- **The COVID-19 Pandemic (2020–):** The pandemic disrupted global economies, exposing the fragility of supply chains and financial systems. Governments worldwide implemented unprecedented fiscal and monetary measures, such as stimulus packages and emergency lending programs, to mitigate economic fallout and support recovery.

These examples demonstrate the necessity of resilience mechanisms, including regulatory frameworks, contingency planning, and international cooperation, in mitigating the impact of financial shocks.

Principles of Financial Resilience

Building financial resilience requires adherence to key principles:

- **Diversification:** Spreading investments and risks across asset classes, industries, and geographies reduces vulnerability to localized shocks. For example, diversified investment portfolios are less susceptible to sector-specific downturns, providing stability during periods of market volatility. Diversification also ensures that economies reliant on specific exports or industries are better protected against global market fluctuations.

- **Liquidity:** Maintaining access to liquid assets ensures that individuals and institutions can meet short-term obligations during crises. Central banks play a crucial role by acting as lenders of last resort and ensuring the availability of liquidity in financial markets. For businesses, liquidity management can be achieved by maintaining cash reserves and optimizing supply chain finance.

- **Adaptability:** The ability to respond swiftly to changing circumstances is essential for resilience. Institutions must invest in technologies and processes that enable real-time decision-making and risk assessment. Adaptive financial systems can quickly reallocate resources to mitigate emerging threats, ensuring that shocks do not escalate into crises.

- **Regulatory Oversight:** Strong regulatory frameworks protect financial systems from systemic risks. By enforcing transparency, accountability, and prudential standards, regulators ensure the stability and integrity of markets. Continuous updates to regulations in response to new challenges, such as digital currencies and climate risks, are necessary to maintain relevance.

- **Collaboration:** Resilience is enhanced through collaboration among governments, financial institutions, and international organizations. Coordinated responses to crises, such as the G20's actions during the 2008 financial crisis, demonstrate the power of collective action in mitigating risks. Collaborative approaches also promote knowledge-sharing and innovation across sectors and borders.

Innovations Enhancing Resilience

Technological advancements and innovative practices are transforming how financial resilience is achieved:

- **Blockchain Technology:** Blockchain's decentralized and immutable nature enhances transparency and security in financial transactions. By reducing reliance on intermediaries and increasing trust, blockchain can bolster resilience in areas such as cross-border payments and supply chain finance. Its potential to track and verify financial transactions in real time adds a layer of trust and security to global financial networks.

- **Artificial Intelligence (AI):** AI-driven risk management tools enable institutions to identify vulnerabilities and respond proactively to emerging threats. Predictive analytics and machine learning algorithms provide real-time insights into market trends and potential disruptions. AI also aids in fraud detection and operational efficiency, allowing institutions to adapt swiftly during periods of volatility.

- **Sustainable Finance:** Integrating environmental, social, and governance (ESG) factors into financial decision-making promotes long-term stability. Sustainable finance initiatives, such as green bonds and impact investing, address systemic risks associated with climate change and social inequality. These approaches align financial goals with broader societal and environmental objectives, creating more resilient systems.

- **Digital Reserves and CBDCs:** Central bank digital currencies (CBDCs) offer a modern approach to enhancing liquidity and financial inclusion. By providing secure and accessible digital payment systems, CBDCs can improve resilience during economic disruptions. Their integration with traditional banking systems ensures smooth transitions during crises.

Case Studies: Resilience in Practice

Several examples illustrate the application of resilience principles:

- **Singapore's Financial System:** Singapore's proactive regulatory environment and robust financial infrastructure have made it one of the most resilient economies globally. Initiatives such as the Monetary Authority of Singapore's (MAS) regulatory sandbox encourage innovation while maintaining stability. The city-state's emphasis on financial education and public-private partnerships further strengthens its resilience.

- **The European Union's Recovery Fund:** In response to the COVID-19 pandemic, the EU established a €750 billion recovery fund to support member states. This coordinated fiscal response highlighted the importance of solidarity and shared resources in building resilience. By targeting investments in green and digital transitions, the fund addresses both immediate recovery and long-term sustainability.

- **Microfinance in Bangladesh:** Microfinance institutions like Grameen Bank have demonstrated the resilience of community-based financial systems. By providing small loans and savings mechanisms, they empower individuals and communities to recover from economic setbacks. These programs have shown remarkable success in lifting people out of poverty and fostering economic self-reliance.

Challenges to Financial Resilience

Despite advancements, significant challenges remain:

- **Global Inequality:** Disparities in wealth and access to resources hinder resilience in developing economies. Addressing inequality requires targeted investments in education, infrastructure, and healthcare to create a foundation for economic stability. Ensuring equitable access to financial services is a critical component of this effort.

- **Climate Change:** Environmental risks, from natural disasters to resource scarcity, pose long-term threats to financial systems. Integrating climate risk assessments into financial planning is essential for safeguarding resilience. Governments and institutions must collaborate on global strategies to mitigate and adapt to these risks.

- **Technological Vulnerabilities:** While technology enhances resilience, it also introduces new risks, such as cyberattacks and data breaches. Strengthening cybersecurity and fostering innovation in secure technologies are critical priorities. Ensuring redundancy and fail-safes in technological infrastructure can further reduce vulnerabilities.

- **Political Uncertainty:** Geopolitical tensions and policy shifts can disrupt markets and undermine confidence. Strengthening international cooperation and promoting stable governance frameworks are key to mitigating these risks. Diplomatic efforts to de-escalate conflicts and foster global economic collaboration are vital.

Additional Insights: Education and Behavioral Adaptation

An often-overlooked aspect of financial resilience is the role of education and behavioral adaptation. Financial literacy programs empower individuals to make informed decisions during times of uncertainty. By understanding concepts such as risk diversification, emergency savings, and credit management, people are better equipped to navigate financial shocks.

Behavioral changes, such as fostering a culture of savings and long-term planning, can also enhance resilience. Encouraging businesses and individuals to adopt proactive financial habits, including creating emergency funds and exploring insurance options, builds a buffer against unforeseen challenges.

Conclusion: Building a Resilient Future

Financial resilience is not a static goal but an ongoing process that requires vigilance, innovation, and collaboration. By embracing principles of diversification, liquidity, adaptability, regulatory oversight, and collaboration, stakeholders can mitigate risks and foster stability in an uncertain world.

The future of financial resilience will depend on our ability to harness technological advancements, address systemic challenges, and promote inclusivity. Policymakers, institutions, and individuals must work together to build financial systems that are not only robust but also equitable and sustainable.

In navigating the complexities of an interconnected global economy, resilience offers a pathway to enduring stability and prosperity. By preparing for the unexpected and fostering collective action, we can ensure that financial systems remain a cornerstone of human progress, capable of weathering the storms of an unpredictable future.

Afterword

As we conclude this book, our goal has been not only to provide you with a deeper understanding of the complex and ever-evolving world of finance but also to present a vision for the future. Money is far more than a medium of exchange; it is a reflection of our values, our society, and our technological progress. The dynamics we have discussed are not static—they continue to evolve and challenge us to adapt and grow with them.

The future of money is in our hands. Whether it involves leveraging innovative technologies like blockchain, building financial resilience in a globalized world, or embedding ethical principles into our economic decisions, we all have the opportunity to actively shape this future.

This book is not intended to be an endpoint but rather a starting point for conversations, reflections, and actions. We invite you to delve deeper into these topics, ask questions, and seek solutions. Dialogue is crucial for creating a world where finance is not only efficient but also fair, sustainable, and inclusive.

If you have questions, suggestions, or feedback, we would be delighted to hear from you. You can reach us anytime at EMBrooksGroup@gmail.com. Your thoughts and perspectives matter to us, and we look forward to hearing from you.

Thank you for embarking on this journey with us. May this book help you better understand the possibilities of the future and actively participate in shaping it.

www.ingramcontent.com/pod-product-compliance
Lightning Source LLC
Chambersburg PA
CBHW031441210526
45464CB00005B/2295